STEPPING STONES TO FREEDOM

# Stepping Stones to Freedom

## A 40 DAY DEVOTIONAL

# Rachel Hickson

MONARCH
BOOKS

Oxford, UK, & Grand Rapids, Michigan

First published in the UK in 2009 by Monarch Books
(a publishing imprint of Lion Hudson plc),
Wilkinson House, Jordan Hill Road, Oxford OX2 8DR.
Tel: +44 (0)1865 302750 Fax: +44 (0)1865 302757
Email: monarch@lionhudson.com
www.lionhudson.com

ISBN: 978-1-85424-895-4 (UK)
ISBN: 978-0-8254-6299-3 (USA)

Distributed by:
UK: Marston Book Services Ltd, PO Box 269, Abingdon, Oxon OX14 4YN;
USA: Kregel Publications, PO Box 2607, Grand Rapids, Michigan 49501

Unless otherwise stated, Scripture quotations are taken from the Holy Bible, New International Version, © 1973, 1978, 1984 by the International Bible Society. Used by permission of Hodder & Stoughton Ltd. All rights reserved.

Photographs courtesy of: Bill Bain, Roger Chouler, Simon Cox, Estelle Lobban, Nick Rous, Stock Xchange.

This book has been printed on paper and board independently certified as having come from sustainable forests.

**British Library Cataloguing Data**
A catalogue record for this book is available from the British Library.

Printed and bound in China.

## Dedication

I dedicate this book to Helen Azer,
my ministry partner and friend,
who has helped me discover these
stepping stones to freedom
as we studied the word together.
Thank you, Helen!

# Contents

## Acknowledgments

This is the part of the book where I want to include everyone, and I am always terrified that I will forget someone important! As always, I want to thank my precious family for releasing me to write. They are great and such an encouragement to me!

I also want to thank Tony Collins, of Monarch, for his easy manner and encouraging attitude as we have discussed how to publish this book. It has been a joy to work with you – thank you!

I also owe a debt of thanks to Helen Azer. She has proofread the text, examined my spelling, corrected my grammar and helped me sound intelligent. Thank you for all your reading time!

Finally, thank *you* for buying this book. I hope it will be a catalyst that will rekindle your dreams and stir up a fresh hunger for God and His word, so that you can enjoy your life with a greater sense of passion and purpose.


Rachel Hickson

# Introduction

*Blessed are those whose strength is in you, who have set their hearts on pilgrimage*

**PSALM 84:5 NIV**

This set of meditations has been written to help you rediscover your purpose in life and activate your desire to discover who you truly are. So you need to set your heart on a pilgrimage of discovery and make the decision that you will allow the word of God to change the way you think about yourself and your future. Maybe you have just been through a tough time when all your dreams have been shattered: your husband has left you, your children are not doing well in school, your boss is overbearing and unsupportive, your finances are in a mess. Whatever the issue, you have lost your connection with God and your sense of perspective in life. This set of notes has been written for people who feel too tired to read the Bible for themselves but know they need to hear God speak. They will help you hear the sound of God in your life again.

Experts tell us that it takes three weeks to start a new habit and six weeks to establish a new way of thinking. So, this will be forty days or six weeks of 'medicine' from the word of God specifically designed to help you discover the true language of your heart in this season of your life. For many of us this authentic language has been crushed. I believe that as you wash your mind with His word, you will begin to identify your true destiny. As you spend time in the word of God, I believe you will renew your mind and bring your spoken words into alignment with the sound of heaven over your life.

So let us pray:

'Father, I believe that as I take these words as medicine every day, just like vitamin tonic, the word of God will do its work in my life and make me strong in my body, mind, soul, spirit and being.

'Father, I trust You to strengthen me and bring change in my life so that I can do the things You ask me to do, say the things You ask me to say, and live the life You ask me to live.

'Thank You, Father, for taking me on this journey of change.

Today I set my heart on this pilgrimage! Thank You, Father! Amen.'

So what is the next step? These meditations have been written as a forty-day series, with a new focus for each week. Each of these topics is a stepping stone on your journey of discovery where God will challenge and renew your way of thinking in an area of your life. The six stepping stones of discovery are as follows:

1. Redeemed and precious
2. Rediscover the leader
3. Reclaim hope
4. Reform your thinking
5. Reawaken your dreams
6. Revive your life

Each day we will read a scripture, meditate on a thought of transformation and then pray a prayer of declaration. You should do this several times – more than once a day if possible – and so let the word do its work by washing your ways of thinking, and changing you. Then at the end of each week take time to re-read all of that week's daily notes together. Let these words just keep washing over you until you know your spirit has grasped the power of this truth in your life.

I believe that as you do this, you will watch the word of God begin to redeem you and help you rediscover the true facets of your inner desire and being. The word will recover and take back what the enemy has stolen, it will realign your way of thinking, it will stir and agitate your dreams again and you will walk out with your life revived!

So read, pray and speak out these words over your life and watch your life be healed as His word does its work!

Thank you so much for walking this journey of change.

Rachel Hickson

# STEPPING STONE 1
## Redeemed and Precious

# Day 1

*But now, this is what the Lord says – he who created you, O Jacob, he who formed you, O Israel: 'Fear not, for I have redeemed you; I have summoned you by name; you are mine. When you pass through the waters, I will be with you; and when you pass through the rivers, they will not sweep over you. When you walk through the fire, you will not be burned; the flames will not set you ablaze. For I am the Lord, your God, the Holy One of Israel, your Saviour; I give Egypt for your ransom, Cush and Seba in your stead. Since you are precious and honoured in my sight, and because I love you, I will give men in exchange for you, and people in exchange for your life. Do not be afraid, for I am with you...'*

**ISAIAH 43:1–5 NIV**

## Thought of transformation

Today God takes hold of your hand. He takes your face in His hands, and He speaks into the depth of your being that you are of great value. Often we feel that bad things only happen to bad people. So when bad things start happening to us, we feel that we must be bad. But when we are walking through the fire of criticism, or being swept away by the waters

of sickness or debt, God promises us that He is with us and these circumstances will not defeat us. He created us and so He knows our capacity and He will help us! But He does not just tolerate us in these difficult seasons of our life, He delights in us! So today let Him speak over you that you are precious, that you *are* loved and you are valued. God loves you. You are not in a difficult place because God does not care!

## Prayer of declaration

So, Father, I thank You that You have redeemed me and You are with me to strengthen and hold me through every trial and difficult place. I thank You that whatever I feel, You never let go and You have redeemed me and will hold me today and every day. You always keep me close and You are the safe place! So, Father, today I pray that I will be more and more aware of the sense of value that You place on my life. Help me overcome every negative attitude that says I deserve this hard place. Pick me up and hold me close and let me hear the sound of 'precious' and 'valued' through my life. Thank You, Father, that You love me! Amen.

# Day 2

> *The Lord himself goes before you and will be with you; he will never leave you nor forsake you. Do not be afraid; do not be discouraged.*
>
> **DEUTERONOMY 31:8 NIV**

## Thought of transformation

The feeling of abandonment can so quickly overshadow our emotions when our circumstances do not feel secure. We can feel alone and vulnerable. Everything seems to shout at us that nobody notices us and therefore nobody cares. But in the midst of all these sounds that seem so real, we must hear the voice of God saying to us: 'I am with you. I *do* go before you. I will never leave you.' Most of us experience the horror of betrayal at some level in our lives. Friends leave us or people break our trust and humiliate us, but we must not lose the truth of His voice: 'I am still with you!' So do not let the fear of isolation grip you. We must realize that these fears are just shadows. God is our reality and He is with us. Do not get discouraged but today allow yourself to be overwhelmed by the encouragement of God. He will *never* leave you! So do not let fear have any hold on

your life. Remember you have the biggest Daddy in the world, and He *never* leaves you, so you can know that you are perfectly safe!

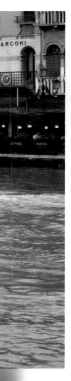

## Prayer of declaration

Father, I thank You that right now I know that I am *never* alone. From the moment You made me, You have watched me and You walk with me all the time. So, Father, I will not be afraid, I will not fear the feeling of abandonment and isolation. Let me know in a new way that You are with me in everyday life. I thank You that I will not be alone. Today I also ask You to fill me with the sound of affirmation and encouragement. I will not be discouraged. I thank You that You will open doors of opportunity and friendship for me and I will not have to live in fear. Father, I find that with You my life increases in vitality and You satisfy me. I will trust You. Thank You that I do not need to face life on my own, because You are with me always! Amen.

# Day 3

*Yet if you devote your heart to him and stretch out your hands to him, if you put away the sin that is in your hand and allow no evil to dwell in your tent, then you will lift up your face without shame; you will stand firm and without fear. You will surely forget your trouble, recalling it only as waters gone by. Life will be brighter than noonday, and darkness will become like morning. You will be secure, because there is hope; you will look about you and take your rest in safety. You will lie down, with no one to make you afraid, and many will court your favour.*

**JOB 11:13–19 NIV**

## Thought of transformation

If we totally give our heart to Him and deal with every poor choice that robs us of our connection with God, then we can live life completely secure. So today God asks you: 'Will you let *go* and let God have complete control? Will you trust Him?' So often we cling to our sinful choices, as we do not really believe that God will fill the gap. But God asks you today to let *go*, and let God fill every empty place. If we will let go, then God will secure us, free us and position us. It will bring such a transformation! Our life can be changed, the trouble that haunted us will be gone and our dark fears will turn into hope and expectation.

When we gamble our lives on the goodness of God, we never lose! There will be a new sense of hope; the old fears will be gone. But the change will be so complete that people will seek to be with you and will want to know what has happened, and they will seek your advice and favour. The change that God brings can turn the negatives into positives; turn the darkness into light; turn the barren places into fruitful harvests; change impossible circumstances into possible situations once again. This God is able to lift your head with hope once again.

## Prayer of declaration

I thank You, Father, that this is my season of change
and You are making me secure. Help me, Lord, to
give You my heart totally and restore trust to me
where I have become withholding. Let me empty
my hands of all the poor choices that I have made –
forgive me and cleanse me, I ask. I know that this is
the season to lift up my head and be secure. I know
that there is a new hope rising and You desire that I
feel safe. I declare that God is with me and so I can
delight in Him. I resist all fear and every atmosphere
of control that limits me and my expression of life.
I declare that I carry favour everywhere I go. I am
secure – I will walk in the light!

# Day 4

*He who dwells in the shelter of the Most High will rest in the shadow of the Almighty. I will say of the Lord, 'He is my refuge and my fortress, my God, in whom I trust.' Surely he will save you from the fowler's snare and from the deadly pestilence. He will cover you with his feathers, and under*  *his wings you will find refuge; his faithfulness will be your shield and rampart. You will not fear the terror of night, nor the arrow that flies by day.*

**PSALM 91:1–5 NIV**

## Thought of transformation

Today God wants you to have a revelation of how to dwell in and occupy this new season of belonging. He wants you to know how to rest and have security as part of your new nature. To dwell literally means

to find a place where you are able to make yourself comfortable and settle. A good picture of this type of 'dwelling' is illustrated by a dog that wanders through the house and then finds a warm place in the sun. The dog then walks round and round before he slumps down and lies in a tight ball and goes to sleep, and so he makes himself a 'dwelling-place'. So often our fears and insecurity keep us agitated all the time, and so even when we are standing still, our mind is restless.

But God challenges us today to find a dwelling-place in Him. He calls us to hide in *Him* and to combat every fear with a declaration that God is our shelter and safe place. We need such a revelation that God is big enough to redeem us from the greatest snares that try to grasp our lives. Our God is able to rescue and save us! But not only does God rescue us, He then protects us and provides us with a sheltered and safe environment to live and dwell in. Our God is able to shield and defend us. We do not need to be afraid, whether it is night or day, as God is aware of us every hour and He does protect us. So today rest, and allow the wing of God to cover you, and dwell in this safe place.

## Prayer of declaration

I thank You, Father, that You are my safe place
where I can dwell. Teach me to hide in You so that
I can develop and mature into all I should be as
I shelter under the wing of God.
Thank You that You will cover me
with Your protection and You will
allow all my dreams to incubate
and grow in this safe place. Father,
I trust You to keep me safe and
secure in this secret place. Father,
I will no longer fear the night-
time, as I know You are with me!
Teach me to rest and dwell in the
knowledge of my Father God who
watches over me night and day.

Thank You for the care and value You give to me.
Teach me a new level of trust, Jesus. Amen.

# Day 5

*The Lord is my shepherd; I shall not be in want. He makes me lie down in green pastures, he leads me beside quiet waters, he restores my soul. He guides me in paths of righteousness for his name's sake. Even though I walk through the valley of the shadow of death, I will fear no evil, for you are with me; your rod and your staff, they comfort me.*

**PSALM 23:1–4 NIV**

## Thought of transformation

As God begins to teach you to rest, you will also need to learn to trust. God wants to be a Shepherd to you, He wants to lead you and direct your life. But you must believe that He is a *good* Shepherd. If you will listen to the sound of His voice in your life, you will not lack any good thing, right from the practical level through to the emotional, intellectual and spiritual dimensions too. This Shepherd can help you organize your world! He will teach you to recognize your rhythms of life too: when you need to take a break and withdraw to recharge, or when you need to stand and battle through circumstances. He knows how you are wired and He can direct your steps so that you never miss the purpose of God in your life, if you will follow His instruction.

We need to learn how to lie down and let our souls be healed after times when we have been wounded, but we also need to know how to walk *through* the troubled seasons of our soul and win. Too often we are overwhelmed and do not walk through the tough times and overcome. But God has made you able to overcome in the valley of the shadow of death, so you need to walk through the season, engage and win! So whatever the circumstances you face, trust the hand of the Shepherd today and let Him guide you.

## Prayer of declaration

Father, I thank You for the hand of the Shepherd in my life. Teach me to trust its touch. I know that I will never lack anything in body, mind or spirit because You will lead and guide me. So, Father, teach me to listen to the sound of Your voice and follow You. I know You are leading me to a place where I can be whole. Please, Father, heal my soul – cleanse me – touch my wounded places and heal the brokenness. I yield to You because You are a *good* Shepherd, so I know that I am safe in Your hands. I will not fear the valleys and the shadows, as I know You will lead me through and teach me to overcome! I thank You, Father, that You are my Shepherd and You know me. Amen.

# Day 6

*The word of the Lord came to me, saying, 'Before I formed you in the womb I knew you, before you were born I set you apart; I appointed you as a prophet to the nations.'*

*'Ah, Sovereign Lord,' I said, 'I do not know how to speak; I am only a child.'*

**JEREMIAH 1:4–6 NIV**

## Thought of transformation

Remember that God was intimately involved in your creation. He is not a remote God who consented to your creation from a great distance. He is like a Potter who put His hands into the clay and made your innermost parts, so He knows your strengths and weaknesses. God placed His fingerprints on the inside of you. He made you for purpose, and you have a unique sound and blend of gifting, and He loves the colour of your life! Not only did He make you, but He also gave you a call and a purpose. Even before He designed the outer vessel, God knew the purpose you would carry in your generation. There are no accidents with God. There are no rejects and no second attempts. Even before you knew what the passions of your heart were, God designated your

appointment. Before you were even born again, God had already planted the embryo seed of destiny in your being, so that when you gave your life to Him, His breath then activated this call.

So now let God redeem these desires for His kingdom. Give Him everything you have and trust Him to satisfy your hidden dreams. Do not let your sense of failure and inadequacy keep you from fulfilling your destiny. We all feel too small to do what God is asking us to do, but He is a *big God* and He asks us to partner with Him. Let God breathe on you and turn the ordinary into the extraordinary. Let God take the natural and make it supernatural. Remember that He knows you and loves you so, and He has called and commissioned you to carry His name. So let go of everything that hinders you from stepping forward and let God uncover all your hidden destiny and start to live life to the full!

## Prayer of declaration

God, I thank You that You know me and have created me with all my gifts, abilities and dreams. Even though You know all my fears and weaknesses, I thank You that You still trust me to partner with You in the kingdom. Help me push through all my excuses and enable me to totally express my personality and destiny. Father, today I decide to accept and honour the person You have made me to be. Teach me to live free from every sense of apology for who I am! Father, I do thank You for creating me – teach me to value this gift of life. Amen.

## Day 7

*O Lord, you have searched me and you know me. You know when I sit and when I rise; you perceive my thoughts from afar. You discern my going out and my lying down; you are familiar with all my ways. Before a word is on my tongue you know it completely, O Lord. You hem me in – behind and before; you have laid your hand upon me. Such knowledge is too wonderful for me, too lofty for me to attain. Where can I go from your Spirit? Where can I flee from your presence? If I go up to the heavens, you are there; if I make my bed in the depths, you are there. If I rise on the wings of the dawn, if I settle on the far side of the sea, even there your hand will guide me, your right hand will hold me fast. If I say, 'Surely the darkness will hide me and the light become night around me,' even the darkness will not be dark to you; the night will shine like the day, for darkness is as light to you. For you created my inmost being; you knit me together in my mother's womb. I praise you because I am fearfully and wonderfully made; your works are wonderful, I know that full well. My frame was not hidden from you when I was made in the secret place. When I was woven together in the depths of the earth, your eyes saw my unformed body. All the days ordained for me were written in your book before one of them came to be. How precious to me are your thoughts,*

*O God! How vast is the sum of them! Were I to count them, they would outnumber the grains of sand. When I awake, I am still with you.*

**PSALM 139:1–18 NIV**

## Thought of transformation

At the end of this first week there is such a need for us to grasp how precious we are to God. Life so often makes us feel that we are just an insignificant face in a huge crowd. But the truth is that God knows the number of the very hairs on our head, and He

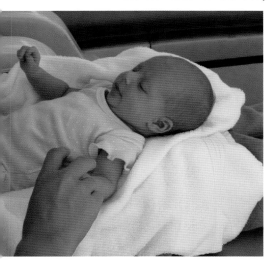

is thinking about us, and these thoughts are good! We can never escape from the affection and love of our God. We are so precious to Him. So let the magnitude of this love touch you deeply today. This is the truth! You are never alone, but rather, you are known to the depth of your being. You are a treasure, precious and valuable to God.

## Prayer of declaration

Thank You, Father, that when I am awake or sleeping, working or resting, You are always there with me. You know me inside out and outside in, and You treasure me! You are good to me and I will rest in You. I am redeemed and precious in Your sight. I am safe and secure. I am loved and precious and made by the King of Kings. Father, I will walk into my entire destiny and be who You made me to be without fear! I am loved and I will walk free. Thank You, Father! Amen.

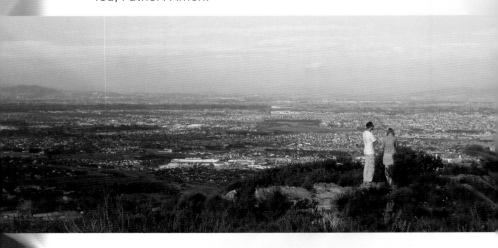

# STEPPING STONE 2
## Rediscover the Leader

# Day 8

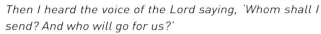

*Then I heard the voice of the Lord saying, 'Whom shall I send? And who will go for us?'*
*And I said, 'Here am I. Send me!'*
*He said, 'Go and tell this people...'*

**ISAIAH 6:8–9 NIV**

## Thought of transformation

Maybe you look at this topic and immediately disqualify yourself. You feel that you are not a leader. But all of us have the power of leadership and we are directing and influencing people with our words and attitudes without even realizing what we are doing. So we need to hear the voice of God directing us first, so that we can guide others around us wisely. We need to hear what God is saying for our children above our natural desires; we need to know what God wants for our business above the sound of our need for success.

So today we need to hear the voice of God calling us and sending us. God will give us a focus outside of ourselves. He will show us the lost and the broken. Once we know that we are loved unconditionally by Him, He then asks us to carry this

love into the world around us. Once we have been healed and forgiven, a new sense of urgency rises in our heart that cries, 'Now send me – I have to go and tell someone the good news that has happened in my life!' God begins to give us a message and a mission, and we begin to lead and influence others with our good news! God loves our availability more than our ability, God delights in our obedience more than our experience.

So let the cry deep within your heart seek God and ask Him to use you. He has made you. He has redeemed you and He can use you! So often we hide in our sense of inadequacy, but God knows that He can take the weakest vessel and make it strong, if we will yield to the Potter's hand. So will you let go and let God use your life?

## Prayer of declaration

Father, I thank You that You have called me and I have felt Your call in my life. Today I acknowledge Your hand of blessing upon my life and realize that I can be a leader of those who are distressed and lead them into a place of peace. So, Father, as I see Your hand of redemption on my life, help me to be one who gives my life away to help others. So today I say to You, Lord: Send me – let me be one who carries Your heart for people and Your message for others. Here I am, Lord. Make me a leader, and I trust You to direct me and teach me what to say. I yield my life to You for Your purposes, God – use me. Amen!

# Day 9

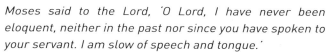

> Moses said to the Lord, 'O Lord, I have never been
> eloquent, neither in the past nor since you have spoken to
> your servant. I am slow of speech and tongue.'
>
> The Lord said to him, 'Who gave man his mouth? Who
> makes him deaf or mute? Who gives him sight or makes
> him blind? Is it not I, the Lord? Now go; I will help you
> speak and will teach you what to say.'
>
> But Moses said, 'O Lord, please send someone else
> to do it.'

**EXODUS 4:10–13 NIV**

## Thought of transformation

I remember when God first challenged me to speak
in public I felt totally horrified. All I could remember
was my struggle to read out loud in class and the
humiliation I felt every time it was my turn. But
God began to confront me, asking me to break the
sound barrier of all my terror and intimidation. He
challenged my well-argued excuses and asked me
if I would rather obey Him or my fears! Finally I
sounded like Moses and surrendered, saying, 'God, I
don't think I can speak very well, but if you are willing
to risk using me, I am willing to be used!'

The amazing thing I discovered is that God is able to take our words and make them sound intelligent and relevant to those who listen. God can transform our communication and make it supernatural, penetrating the deep heart-cries of people around us. God's word in our mouth has great power but we need to open our mouth and let Him speak. God wants us to realize that He holds the keys to all creative power and He can transform our ability to speak and communicate and make us instruments of power in His hands. He is able to take nothing and make something; He is able to craft our tongues to be His instrument of blessing and freedom.

So this passage instructs us that we must not allow our sense of failure and weakness to limit God's creative power that wants to work through our lives. We must not miss our destiny because we allow fear to rule our mouths.

## Prayer of declaration

Lord, I am sorry for the times when I have allowed fear to stop me speaking, when I have known that I should speak. I am sorry that I have not trusted You to give me the right words at the right time. I know that even when I do not feel adequately prepared, You still have the power to give me all the information that I need. Thank You, Lord, that Your creative hand upon my life enables me to be a communicator. Thank You for every time You will use my mouth as Your instrument. Lord, I do want You to use me and I am sorry for the times I have said I want to be somewhere else or I have asked You to use someone else. Lord, here I am – make me Your mouthpiece. Amen.

# Day 10

*Moses said to the Lord, 'You have been telling me, "Lead these people," but you have not let me know whom you will send with me. You have said, "I know you by name and you have found favour with me." If you are pleased with me, teach me your ways so I may know you and continue to find favour with you. Remember that this nation is your people.'*

*The Lord replied, 'My Presence will go with you, and I will give you rest.'*

*Then Moses said to him, 'If your Presence does not go with us, do not send us up from here. How will anyone know that you are pleased with me and with your people unless you go with us? What else will distinguish me and your people from all the other people on the face of the earth?'*

**EXODUS 33:12–16 NIV**

## Thought of transformation

In this season of your life God is asking you to step out of your comfort zones and to influence the lives of people around you. But as we accept this challenge, we realize that we need a deeper level of relationship with God so that people around us know that it is God

speaking and not us. Suddenly we need people to know that God is our greatest treasure and He is the one who has changed our world. I remember being asked once what the brand of the makeup that I wore was. The shop assistant had commented that my face had a very clear but special glow and wanted to know what I had used to gain such a fine texture. However, I was not wearing any makeup that day, but I had just come from a service where I had really been touched by the love of God.

This was the cry of Moses. He wanted people around him to notice that he was different because he had been with God. Like Moses, we want to be glory carriers in our generation so that when people watch our lives, they recognize that we are different. We want people to notice that there is a special atmosphere of favour around us and that we are blessed. We need to be the marked-out generation that carries an atmosphere of generosity and gratitude. People need to know that this is not our nice personality but that we have been marked out by God. We need to be those who carry a heavy presence of God's peace and rest into every situation. We need to change the atmosphere of our workplaces and universities and be glory carriers in this dark generation.

## Prayer of declaration

Father, I am asking You today to mark me with Your presence. I want to be a leader who knows the sense of the glory of God upon my life at all times. God, I want to know that You rest on my life and that

I can know this rest as I lead. I thank You that I do not need to be weary and stressed but I can know peace and rest. Mark me with Your presence and let me know Your kiss of glory touching my life. Thank You! Amen.

# Day 11

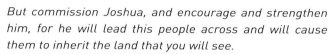

*But commission Joshua, and encourage and strengthen him, for he will lead this people across and will cause them to inherit the land that you will see.*

**DEUTERONOMY 3:28 NIV**

## Thought of transformation

Encouragement and affirmation are powerful atmospheres that help us grow into our full potential. However, too often we quickly dismiss these positive words of hope and then readily receive the negative comments of criticism. So, today, take a moment to think and meditate on the words of encouragement that have been spoken over your life. These words have the power of life and will help you keep a correct perspective of who you are and what you are called to do. We need to resist the effects of accusation and rejection in our lives, as these atmospheres will always distract us from our purpose.

So keep rebuilding your spirit with the words of life. As you build yourself up in the truth, you will be able to lead others into their inheritance too. You will find that you are able to recognize their calling, their strengths and gifting, and then you can use your

mouth to speak words of strength into their destiny. So today, remind yourself whose you are and what you are in God, and then encourage yourself in your ability to do what He has asked you to do. Then ask God to commission you to lead others into their destiny and call. Today, be someone who speaks life into people's destiny and help others grow as you surround them with an atmosphere of love and hope.

## Prayer of declaration

Father, please give me people in my life who will strengthen and encourage the leader in me by speaking words of affirmation that encourage me. Please protect my back from all negative criticism so that I feel secure and protected. Father, as I encourage people to grasp their promises and inheritance, I ask that You will give me wisdom and strength. I want to help people discover the place of satisfaction and fulfilment in their lives. Please give me the right words for their lives. I believe that You have commissioned me with new hope and I believe that as I step out, I will receive all the encouragement and strength that I need from You and others. So, Father, I thank You for strengthening me to live my life to the full. I receive my strength from You. Amen.

# Day 12

*'Go,' the Lord said to me, 'and lead the people on their way, so that they may enter and possess the land that I swore to their fathers to give them.' And now, what does the Lord your God ask of you but to fear the Lord your God, to walk in all his ways, to love him, to serve the Lord your God with all your heart and with all your soul, and to observe the Lord's commands and decrees that I am giving you today for your own good?*

**DEUTERONOMY 10:11–13 NIV**

## Thought of transformation

As we begin to allow God to use our life to touch others around us, we need to ensure that we keep hungry for God. It is so easy to get very busy helping others and then forget that we need to keep ourselves in the yielded place where God can touch the depths of our attitudes and emotions. As we allow our confidence to return, we must not let the enemy have any room to come and accuse us of our past – otherwise we may make poor choices about how we live today. So decide to cultivate the fear of the Lord in your life. This does not mean that you live in terror of Him, but rather that you have a passion to live your life

blessing God in all the little things. In other words, because of your honour and love for Him, you will consistently choose to do what blesses God, as you 'fear' the possibility that your life could be a cause of disappointment to Him. It is the same motivation as that of young lovers! You will go anywhere, look through countless stores to find the right gift, stay up all night or drive miles to support and help your partner, just because you love greatly and you do not want to disappoint the new love in your life!

So God asks us to live a life with definite choices to bless Him. So we need to renew our way of thinking, refuse all rejection and walk a lifestyle that is genuine from deep inside our heart and soul. We need to learn to be vulnerable lovers who allow people to get close to us, who are able to serve and bless others. We need to respond and obey quickly and do what God asks us to do without fear... We need to walk right!

## Prayer of declaration

So, God, as I step out to lead, I pray that I will qualify with all my heart and life to fulfil this call of leadership. Help me to love Your ways and to serve You with all my heart. Let me never lose my love for You. God, I do not want to do this for myself alone but I want to do this for You... I want to model Your style of leadership and be a person who loves God first and then loves people. Help me to honour You in all I do! Teach me to choose Your way quickly. Let me love You deeply and trust You to use my life to bless You and those around me. Thank You for this love. Amen.

# Day 13

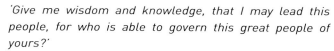

> 'Give me wisdom and knowledge, that I may lead this people, for who is able to govern this great people of yours?'
>
> God said to Solomon, 'Since this is your heart's desire and you have not asked for wealth, riches or honour, nor for the death of your enemies, and since you have not asked for a long life but for wisdom and knowledge to govern my people over whom I have made you king, therefore wisdom and knowledge will be given you. And I will also give you wealth, riches and honour, such as no king who was before you ever had and none after you will have.'

**2 CHRONICLES 1:10–12 NIV**

## Thought of transformation

What are you asking God to give you? So often we only ask for practical and material provisions from God, but today God wants you to ask for things of eternal worth. What do you need in your life to complete your talents and calling so that you can influence and direct your generation more effectively? As you step out into a new confidence that God has a purpose for your life, what are the resources that you need from God to make your life more effective? When we have

54

been through a tough time, it is easy for us to get focused on our needs or even our revenge.

Here God congratulates Solomon that he has not asked for possessions that will give him an elevated status, he has not asked for retaliation and the death of his enemies, but he has asked for gifts that will accelerate his calling and enable him to do what God has asked him to do. Ask God to remind you where you are called to lead, and then seek Him to discover what tools and talents you need to do this task, and then begin to ask God specifically for these gifts. Examine your heart's desire and then express it and let the heart-cry of your inner spirit cry out, and then watch the blessing that God will release into your life.

## Prayer of declaration

Father, I really want to be a good leader with a heart that seeks the right things. Keep me from pursuing importance and reputation, but put in me a deep hunger for spiritual qualities that will enable me to lead correctly. I ask You to teach me all wisdom and to help me be who I should be. God, I do not want to strive for fame. I do not want to live in fear of my reputation, but I want to be wise and help the people that I lead. Father, today I thank You that You have called me to lead and I receive all wisdom and power. I thank You that as I choose You, You choose me and will bless me with all that I need. I will be a leader of both spiritual and natural resources. Thank You for Your provision in my life. Amen.

# Day 14

*Then I will give you shepherds after my own heart, who will lead you with knowledge and understanding.*

**JEREMIAH 3:15 NIV**

## Thought of transformation

This is the season when God wants people to feel loved, cherished and secure. God's priority is always people. He loves people and they are His most precious possession. He is a *good* Shepherd and so He wants to train us to have a heart that responds like His. He wants to place in us genuine compassion for people. He wants shepherds in the community who will respond like Him, who will care for the harassed and helpless, as He does. He wants shepherds who seek out people and are prepared to go into the difficult place to rescue precious souls.

Can you see people and identify with their pain – does the hardship of others affect your life? We need to be shepherds who model our lives after the generous heart of our Father. Then, once we decide to give our life away to the needy and the hurting, we need to ask God to increase our knowledge and understanding so that we can give these people a message of hope. We

need to know the word of God and understand the principles of God, but then we need the specific individual wisdom which brings understanding for each situation. We cannot just have a list of automatic responses to certain circumstances that we use every time we meet people with this need, but rather we need to be shepherds who have specific understanding for each circumstance which has come from the place of prayer. As a mother I have felt so challenged to 'shepherd' my children with knowledge and understanding. I need to have knowledge and then specific revealed wisdom for each challenge.

## Prayer of declaration

Father, at all times, keep my heart soft. Let my heart speak like Yours. Let me think like You when I am with people. God, I know the heart of the matter is the matter of my heart. So I surrender my heart to You and ask You to make me a shepherd who leads with a heart like Yours. I trust You to increase my knowledge and understanding as I correct my heart attitudes. Let me receive my fresh mantle to lead, and I trust You to help me do it well. I am a leader who will influence those in my home, my workplace and my family. Let me lead people into a deep passion for You and Your ways. Amen.

# STEPPING STONE 3
## Reclaim Hope

# Day 15

*I wait for the Lord, my soul waits, and in his word I put my hope. My soul waits for the Lord more than watchmen wait for the morning, more than watchmen wait for the morning. Put your hope in the Lord, for with the Lord is unfailing love and with him is full redemption.*

**PSALM 130:5–7 NIV**

## Thought of transformation

Hope is one of the essential ingredients of a purpose-filled life. In 1 Corinthians 13:13 we read: 'Now these three remain: faith, *hope* and love. But the greatest of these is love.' So, one of the consistent qualities of our life should be hope. It should be a foundational atmosphere of our personality upon which our faith and love depend. But in today's society there is so much hopelessness, and people feel that hope becomes the doorway to disappointment rather than the gateway for our dreams to be achieved. So we need to redeem this attitude of hope and learn to hope in God. We need that eager expectation of hope that is able to look at all our promises and watch and wait for God to show us how these hopes and dreams will become reality.

What is hope? Well, one definition is this: Hope is a God-given desire with a faith-filled expectation of accomplishment. This is why genuine hope is based on God's word or His promise for our life. As we spend time in the word of God and train our soul, that intimate place of our desires, to wait in His presence, our lives will become based on godly desires that trigger genuine hope. So we need to train our emotions to wait and listen for God's sound and purpose for our lives.

I wanted to be a medical doctor working in Nepal with the Leprosy Mission. So as I completed my university applications, I longed and hoped for a place at medical school. When I was refused, all my hopes and dreams crashed and my world collapsed. But then I took some time to wait, and God showed me His purpose. I met Gordon during this time and later we married. I trained in medical research and began to teach. Today I travel the world preaching His word, using these research and teaching skills I learnt in my early days of work. At nineteen I had lost my hope, but today I see that God knew what He was doing, and I have fulfilled more dreams than I thought possible.

So, today, put your hope in God and ask Him to help you purify your hope so that it is based on His word.

## Prayer of declaration

Thank You, Father, for the place of rest and waiting – we do not have to strive, but You will come and meet with us. I thank You that as I wait for You, I will watch and see my hopes and dreams come true. I thank You that as we wait, You are able to heal the places where hopes and dreams have been shattered and give us a new perspective. Today, as I think about this quality of hope, let my desires and longings be reawakened. Remind me of those hopes and promises that You have given me and let me hope again. Teach me, precious Father, to put my hope in You again. I give You all my hopes and desires concerning my life, my relationships, my work and my finances, and I ask You to teach me to hope in You today. Amen.

# Day 16

*There is surely a future hope for you, and your hope will not be cut off.*

**PROVERBS 23:18 NIV**

*'For I know the plans I have for you,' declares the Lord, 'plans to prosper you and not to harm you, plans to give you hope and a future. Then you will call upon me and come and pray to me, and I will listen to you. You will seek me and find me when you seek me with all your heart. I will be found by you,' declares the Lord.*

**JEREMIAH 29:11–14 NIV**

## Thought of transformation

Hope will enable you to have peace concerning your future. As I shared yesterday, at eighteen I thought I knew what my future would look like – serving as a medical doctor in Nepal – but this was based on my personal fears and emotions and had not been birthed from a place of prayer or asking God. Since the goal was Christian work and service, everyone, including me, thought this must be from God. But when it all went wrong, I began to pray and I discovered that God had other plans, but I needed to discover them too!

God has plans for your life and your future, and these plans are secure. There is a hope for your future and these plans will give you satisfaction. The challenge for us is this – we have to discover these plans! God has a plan for your life – it will satisfy every dream and longing; it will give you hope and prosperity; it will satisfy you and your personality.

But we need to take the time to seek and discover this plan for our life. So because we know God has a plan for us, this should stir in our life a new desire to connect with God so that we can understand this plan. So we need to come to a new place of hope that God is in control and that if we will take the time, God will show us these plans and we will know that we are doing the right thing at the right time. God wants to give us his blueprint for our lives, and as we come to Him he will show us these plans. So how do we hear? We need to take time to listen, and we need to trust that our instincts and thoughts, when we listen, are God-triggered. When we ask God to speak and take time to seek Him, I believe the voice and thoughts that we receive in these times originate from God.

Today, so many in our society have lost hope and have no sense of security about their future. There is a weariness and fatigue about tomorrow. Unfortunately, we have seen a rise in suicide rates, especially amongst young people, as this

hopelessness begins to rob them of the hope of a future. But your God loves to give you hope for your tomorrow! So today let the words of God activate a new sense of expectancy about your future. Know that God has all things under control and He has a plan for you.

## Prayer of declaration

Jesus, right now I know that You have every detail and step of my future in Your hands. So I thank You that my future dreams will *not* lead me to disappointment. Father, I thank You that this is Your word over my life: There is surely a future hope for *me*, and *my* hope will not be cut off. I thank You that I can trust You for every step of my life and that You will direct and lead my decisions. Teach me to be more confident that when I ask You to show me my future, I will indeed hear You. Teach me to trust You to direct me and give me the steps I need to take. Father, I thank You for a new hope for my tomorrows! Amen.

# Day 17

*...but those who hope in the Lord will renew their strength. They will soar on wings like eagles; they will run and not grow weary, they will walk and not be faint.*

**ISAIAH 40:31 NIV**

## Thought of transformation

When you feel overwhelmed, where do you find your place of replenishment? So often we find ourselves saying, 'I'm exhausted – I just need a coffee!' But if you know you need extra emotional capacity as you are facing hard times, where do you find your true place of strength? We need to teach ourselves to turn and find God in these times of refreshment and refocus. If we are

people who truly hope in God – if our lives truly lean on the foundation of the goodness of God – then when we need new vision and emotional capacity, we will

67

be God-seekers. Are you able to lean on and hope in God when you need a greater sense of perspective? 'God, I am feeling tired and weary, but as I put my desires and expectations in Your hands, I know this environment strengthens my faith, my knowledge that You are good, and I will break through.'

As we truly hope in God, we find new strength arises as we are able to fill in the gaps that produce worry and fear and so deplete our emotional reserves. Our strength comes from this new certainty of who our God is and that He is able to hold us while we struggle for the breakthrough of our dreams.

As our strength of conviction and faith is secured, we are then able to have a new perspective concerning the issues. We soar above the issues rather than being overwhelmed by them. We soar on those wings of hope, faith and expectation. A new joy awakens and we rise above the sense of hopelessness and find a new vigour to press through. Suddenly, we remember why this situation matters to us and we want to see these promises fulfilled. A new hope and longing awakens and we want to run into the purposes of God with fresh vision. There is a new spring in our step and fresh hope in our hearts. The weariness of the waiting season is broken and you sense the promise of the breakthrough once again.

If we want to truly keep pressing into all our hopes and dreams, then we must keep leaning into God. As we hope in God, we will break the monotony of the waiting season and not get weary and lose hope. If you learn to hope correctly, you will be able to run forward into all your purposes, break the power of weariness and keep moving into your destiny. So today hope in God and learn to soar, fly, run and finish the race!

## Prayer of declaration

So, Jesus, I ask You today to let a new hope arise in me. Let me hope in my God and find new strength. Let this strength awaken my expectation and longing for more. Let me begin to soar again above every atmosphere that keeps me burdened. Take away all the fear of exhaustion and let me know, as I walk in this season of hope, that I *can* run and not be weary! Amen.

# Day 18

*Hope deferred makes the heart sick, but a longing fulfilled is a tree of life.*

**PROVERBS 13:12 NIV**

*Then you will know that I am the Lord; those who hope in me will not be disappointed.*

**ISAIAH 49:23 NIV**

## Thought of transformation

When asked for a scripture about hope, most people in church recite this verse: 'Hope deferred makes the heart sick' – but they rarely complete the verse! As a result, many people feel hope is an unlikely expectation that will only result in pain and disappointment. We seem to have an unwritten proverb in the church: 'Do not hope too much and then you will not be too badly disappointed.' But we have lost the meaning of this verse and the gift of hope! Here we are shown that hope can have two outcomes – either the delay of our hope, which can cause bitterness and disappointment, or the journey of our hope, which can produce the tree of life once the hope has been processed and fulfilled! But hope needs commitment to the journey. Those desires and dreams will have an outcome, but first we have to walk the journey of delay!

So when we think about hope, rather than thinking about the delay and the sick heart that results if we get bitter, we need to remember the other scriptures that promise us that this hope is secure and does not bring disappointment. We need to consider the way we think. Winston Churchill says this in one of his famous quotations: 'The pessimist sees difficulty in every opportunity. The optimist sees the opportunity in every difficulty.' So we need to have this attitude that looks into every opportunity with hope, and we need to live with an expectation that God will come through for us and give us the best.

If we have found that we have become cynical, then we need to ask God to come and give us a new ability to trust and dream again. All of us will encounter circumstances when we are betrayed, where dreams of a wonderful friendship will be broken, or the perfect job does not happen and our hopes are dashed. But out of these seasons we must let hope rise up once again. We need to get a full God-perspective and hope in Him and allow the pain of the season of disappointment to melt away. So we need to ask God to teach us to really know that He is the Lord, and then out of this new confident knowledge

we will also know that those who hope in God will not be disappointed. So I trust that you will feel this new knowledge of God growing, until you can say that you know that you know that you know that God is good and this hope does not disappoint you!

## Prayer of declaration

Jesus, I know that *You* have plans for me, and so I will rest. I thank You that as I seek You, I will find and know these perfect paths. So, Father, help me learn how to come, pray and listen in this new season... Thank You that I *will* be found by You and this rising hope will not disappoint me. I thank You that as my knowledge of You increases, I will find my hopes are fulfilled. Please touch my heart where I have become sick and disappointed and reawaken hope in my spirit again. Thank You! Amen.

# Day 19

*Against all hope, Abraham in hope believed and so became the father of many nations, just as it had been said to him, 'So shall your offspring be'. Without weakening in his faith, he faced the fact that his body was as good as dead – since he was about a hundred years old – and that Sarah's womb was also dead.*

**ROMANS 4:18–19 NIV**

## Thought of transformation

Here we see the courage of Abraham – he hoped against hope! There are seasons in life when all the facts seem to indicate that your dreams are now impossible and your hope is a mere fantasy. But here, even after facing the facts, Abraham found courage and wrestled for his hope.

A few years ago I was challenged to hope against hope by a couple longing for a child. The medical evidence was very negative and they had been trying to conceive for years, but they had a word that God would give them a family. So we prayed, and after prayer, the wife became pregnant. She carried the babies to nearly full term and went into labour, but unfortunately they died shortly after birth. The couple were devastated by their loss and also discovered that their chances of another pregnancy were further reduced due to the complications. But the next time I was in their church in the USA, they asked me to pray for them again. And so through our tears we prayed, and after a delay, the wife became pregnant again, and this time gave birth to a healthy baby girl.

But they still wrestled in hope as they said, 'God promised us a family – not just a baby.' And as we prayed yet again, she became pregnant again and now has delivered another healthy baby girl. All the facts screamed, 'You cannot have a child!' – but they wrestled with their hope against every expectation around them and the word of God proved faithful. It is hard to stand and press through apparent evidence and still believe in the hopes and dreams that God gives you.

Martin Luther King, Jr makes this statement: 'If you lose hope, somehow you lose the vitality that keeps life moving, you lose that courage to be, that quality that helps you go on in spite of it all. And so today I still have a dream.' If we are to keep our hope and dreams then we, too, need to learn to wrestle with our hope and win the battle of courage! Do not let setbacks and time delays destroy your hope. Let hope arise and believe that God always has the final word.

## Prayer of declaration

So, Father, as I look at my life and my capacity and
feel I do not have the strength to wrestle and hope
against hope, I thank You that it is not about *my*
resources, but about *Your* resources. So I believe
that even though I feel my body is dead, I can still
achieve all You have asked me to do. Today I ask You
to give me grace to examine the facts and even see
the futility, but then see a God who is able to step
into my world and answer my cry. Father, I know
that You are able to fulfil Your word over my life.
Like Abraham, help me to still keep believing even
when I am confronted
by negative facts. Give
me courage to hope
against hope. Amen.

# Day 20

> *And we rejoice in the hope of the glory of God. Not only so, but we also rejoice in our sufferings, because we know that suffering produces perseverance; perseverance, character; and character, hope. And hope does not disappoint us, because God has poured out his love into our hearts by the Holy Spirit, whom he has given us.*

**ROMANS 5:2–5 NIV**

## Thought of transformation

So even in this season of battle, we can feel the change of atmosphere. We can begin to rejoice, since we know God is in control. We can have joy as we hope in the fact that God is a breakthrough God and his glory will be seen. But this scripture then challenges us to understand the journey of this breakthrough too. Yes, we will rejoice in the hope of his glory, but we need to understand that this glory is produced by these tough times. Can we find the hope that rejoices in the battle of the journey as much as it rejoices in the victory? Here God challenges us to rejoice when we are going through times of suffering.

I wonder – do we know that we know that we know, in the depth of our beings, that in these

challenging seasons God is not hurting us but developing us for His purpose? These times of struggle produce gold that lasts forever! I remember that after my road-traffic accident in 1984 I learned some of these lessons. I was twenty-four years old and had a six-month-old baby. I had nearly died on the road in Harare, Zimbabwe, but God had healed the brain trauma caused by multi-fat emboli and I had been flown home to the UK to recover. I had fractured both my legs severely and was in a wheelchair and living in constant pain. I had a hope and a word for my full recovery and believed that I would walk again soon. But this journey took nearly four years. I carried this hope in my heart but there were many disappointments as I visited the hospital. My bones took months to form a callus and did not heal, and so I was confined to a wheelchair as my baby grew and learned to walk and run!

At times I could not understand the delay and felt disappointed by God. Did He not want to heal me? Then one day God spoke to me and said, 'Rachel, you have to remember that the process is as important as the product – do not miss the treasure on this journey!' I realized that all I wanted was the product – healed legs – but God was showing me many other treasures on the way, and I had missed these gems! I cried and asked God to help me enjoy the journey too.

Finally, one day in a service, when I was least expecting it, God touched my legs and I was healed, and today I walk without pain. As I stood and cried at that service, God said to me: 'Rachel, I love you, and I wanted to heal this cripple from the inside out!' Remember that this hope *does not* disappoint us, as He has poured out His love for us.

## Prayer of declaration

So, Jesus, even though
some of the journey
has been tough, I know
that there is a purpose and
life is growing from this hard
place. Father, let me see all that
this season has produced in my life – help
me see the journey and have fresh hope that You
work all things for my character and growth... I can
hope that all things are working together for good.
Father, let me know Your love poured out today and
help me focus on the treasure on this journey, until I
see the full glory of the breakthrough. Amen.

# Day 21

*May the God of hope fill you with all joy and peace as you trust in him, so that you may overflow with hope by the power of the Holy Spirit.*

**ROMANS 15:13 NIV**

## Thought of transformation

So today, as we complete this stepping stone of hope, let God activate your desires once again. Let the water of His Spirit soak your life so that the new shoots of hope flourish in your heart. Remember that hope is your God-given desire with a faith-filled sense of expectation that these promises will be fulfilled. So invite God to come and fill you with a fresh sense of joy and peace. Let the joy of the certainty of His promise fill you. But also let peace rule your emotions, let God conquer all the fears that shout, 'Do not hope – you will only be disappointed!'

Let this God of hope fill you!

Today examine your heart and look at those areas where hopelessness and cynicism have dominated your way of thinking, and ask God to change you. Where you have withdrawn, God wants you to overflow. Maybe you have felt you have nothing to offer as you are in such a place of battle, but God can fill you and make you a resource to others. This does not depend on your ability but on His capacity poured into your life. So often I have felt I have nothing to give, but as I have begun to pour out, I have discovered that God has poured into me first!

So as you go out today, ask God to show you someone whom you can touch with this message of hope. I remember, about five years ago, I was in Northern Ireland ministering. I had been ill and had a very sore throat. I wondered how I was going to speak, but I decided I should still go to the next meeting. As I entered the room, coffee was still being served, so I sat with a woman and began to talk to her. She said she had come to this meeting as a final resort. It was her daughter's birthday that day, but her girl had run away from home, was living on drugs and she had not seen her for years.

As she talked of the hopelessness of this situation, I began to cry and then I felt God gave me a word of hope. I said to this woman, 'I believe that your daughter is like the prodigal son. She has come to the end of herself and she wants to come home. Get ready. She will be coming home, and God will show you how to help her.' This woman smiled with a tired smile, and we prayed and she got up and went home.

A few months later I heard that, indeed, the daughter had come home the next day. The mother had been prepared, and now this precious daughter has completed Bible school and is serving God with passion!

Now it's your turn. You will overflow by the power of the Holy Spirit in you, and you will be a messenger of hope in a season of hopelessness for so many.

## Prayer of declaration

So, Jesus, I open my life to You again and ask You to fill me with a fresh outpouring of hope. Please fill me, precious Holy Spirit. I thank You for the sense of all Your joy and peace during this season... Deepen my trust in You and help me know that my life does overflow with You, Jesus. I thank You for the power of the Holy Spirit living in me... Let there be *more* of You, Jesus – fill me with more of You! Teach me to overflow with this hope for others. Let me learn to receive from You and then give this hope away. Let me carry an atmosphere of hope and blessing in my life. Thank You, Father. Amen.

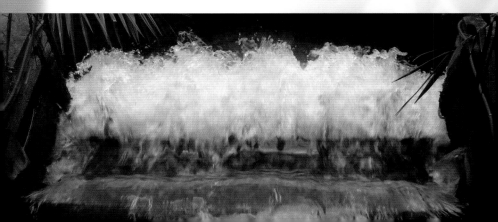

# STEPPING STONE 4
## Reform Your Thinking

# Day 22

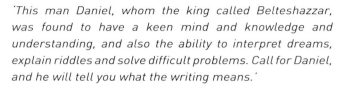

*'This man Daniel, whom the king called Belteshazzar, was found to have a keen mind and knowledge and understanding, and also the ability to interpret dreams, explain riddles and solve difficult problems. Call for Daniel, and he will tell you what the writing means.'*

**DANIEL 5:12 NIV**

## Thought of transformation

So often in the Christian life we are very concerned about our heart issues but not sure what to do with our mind. We can even get the impression from church that our mind is a hindrance to God and that it is more important to feel than to think! But I believe that God wants informed, intelligent people who love Him with all their hearts! Three years ago my husband and I moved to Oxford where we pastor a church in the centre of this university city. We soon discovered that our church was full of incredibly gifted young people with sharp minds. Many of them felt guilty about their intelligence.

But I have also met many people who carry labels from their school days where they were told they were stupid and they would never do anything! In

the press today we read about children with learning difficulties and about the increase of ADD (attention deficit disorder) and dyslexia. But I know God wants to restore our minds and release us from all shame. So if we are going to step into our full destiny, we must allow God to touch and release the capacity of our minds and to heal our hearts.

Recently I was at a conference in Portland, USA, and I offered a time of prayer for those who wanted God to touch their minds – maybe they felt that they had been labelled either 'Geek' (super intelligent) or 'Idiot'. As I finished giving this call, I was amazed as hundreds of people streamed forward, many with tears flowing down their faces. I realized that day that we need to help each other renew our minds and reform our ways of thinking. Usually it is the space between our ears that determines the way our life goes! When the enemy convinces us in our mind that we are stupid, weird or strange, this becomes a doorway for rejection. And so we withdraw, our heart gets damaged, and then we lose our hope and purpose for life.

So today, realize that your mind is a gift from God. Some of us are able to read huge books and speak many languages, others are gifted with creativity and artistic talent, and still others have that gift of common sense and practical logic that saves many people from disasters! But all of us have a mind, and we need to ask God to bless our capacity and help us to stretch our ability and use it for Him.

## Prayer of declaration

Father, I thank You for the intelligence and the creativity that You have given me. I thank You that You have made me able to think clearly, learn information and have knowledge and understanding. I thank You for the gift of my mind and its ability to imagine and create. Right now I bless my capacity to think, learn, design and communicate. Right now I break every fear that says I cannot think, I am unintelligent – or that I will lose my mind or go senile. I thank You that You have created my heart and my mind to work together and that there is no separation. You have made me both able to think and able to feel... Thank You for touching my mind. Amen!

# Day 23

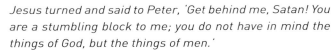

*Jesus turned and said to Peter, 'Get behind me, Satan! You are a stumbling block to me; you do not have in mind the things of God, but the things of men.'*

**MATTHEW 16:23 NIV**

*'For who has known the mind of the Lord that he may instruct him?' But we have the mind of Christ.*

**1 CORINTHIANS 2:16 NIV**

## Thought of transformation

So often our way of thinking can become a hindrance to the purposes of God in our life. Here we read the story where Peter has allowed his natural emotions and logic to direct his decision-making. He did not want Jesus to go to Jerusalem, as it was dangerous. So his natural thinking concluded this must be wrong – so Jesus had to correct him! Most of the processes of deduction that we are taught in our secular education are contrary to the life of faith that we are called to live. The Christian life does not always 'make sense'! So we need to ask God to teach us a new way of decision-making and thinking. We need to learn how to keep in mind the things of God above our human process of analysis.

I remember when God asked us to move to Africa as missionaries, I was very concerned about the finances for this venture. We had sold our car, house and business and we had no adequate monthly support, but knew we had to go. Before we left England God then challenged us to give away our final savings account to a pastor who needed a car. This was the only financial backup we had. It seemed irresponsible to give this money away, as we had a toddler at the time. But we did give it away and left for Africa. Then I became pregnant with my son, David.

The fear of money became a real blockage in my life, until one day God challenged me. 'Rachel,' he asked me, 'do you believe that I reward those who work for Me? Do you believe I can pay for your medical bills to have this baby in Africa? Are you working for Me here in Africa? Do you think I am a good employer?' I cried and asked God to give me his way of thinking concerning finances. Then, within a few days, we received two gifts in the mail that completely paid all our medical bills for the birth of David. God was faithful, and I learnt a lesson of kingdom thinking concerning finances. If God has ordered the project, God will pay for it!

## Prayer of declaration

Father, I thank You that You can teach me to have the right reactions in my way of thinking. I ask You to help me ensure that my mind is saying the same thing as heaven is saying in each situation. God, prevent my mind from becoming a stumbling-block in my life. Father, I ask You to teach me to have the godly way of thinking and not be contained by my rational thought processes. Father, give me the mind of Christ. Father, anoint my mind with Christ-like attitudes so that I think like Him and my mind is never a hindrance but always able to instruct me in God's ways. Help me learn to use my mind for You more and more. Thank You. Amen.

# Day 24

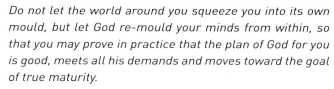

*Do not let the world around you squeeze you into its own mould, but let God re-mould your minds from within, so that you may prove in practice that the plan of God for you is good, meets all his demands and moves toward the goal of true maturity.*

**ROMANS 12:2 J. B. PHILLIPS**

*For though we live in the world, we do not wage war as the world does. The weapons we fight with are not the weapons of the world. On the contrary, they have divine power to demolish strongholds. We demolish arguments and every pretension that sets itself up against the knowledge of God, and we take captive every thought to make it obedient to Christ.*

**2 CORINTHIANS 10:3–5 NIV**

## Thought of transformation

I love the graphic picture painted by the J. B. Phillips translation of Romans 12:2. The peer pressure that influences the way we think is so subtle that often we do not even realize we have moved from our position of faith and purity. Our minds get squeezed! We need to keep washing our minds with the truth of the word of God, or we will quickly lose our life's reference points. Each one of us needs regular brainwashing! It is so easy to allow your thinking to be influenced by the media and to lose your clarity on what is right and wrong. In this culture, where people celebrate no absolute truth, we need to keep soaking our lives in the word of truth.

So we are in a battle for our minds. The battleground for our faith is fought between our ears every day. We need to take the divine power of God and resist the arguments, deceptions and pretences that are contrary to the will and purpose of God in our lives. We need to take captive those thoughts and ways of thinking that contain our destiny and limit our faith. Everything that stirs unbelief and fear needs to be wrestled with in faith so that we do not develop strongholds of thinking that resist the truth of God in our lives. We need to imprison the thoughts that would love to make us the prisoner! It is time to take the power of God and battle for our minds so that we can be free in our thinking!

## Prayer of declaration

So, Father, I thank You that I know I can have the mind of Christ. I ask You now to cleanse all my ways of thinking from every wrong spiritual and natural influence. Will You cleanse my mind from all secularism and rationalism and every religious spirit that offends You? I thank You that You give me power to win the battle of the mind. So I ask You to protect me from all political correctness and peer pressure that influences the way I think. Give me the mind of Christ. Thank You, Father, that I do not need to fight the battle of the mind with natural resources; rather, You give me the power to fight and win. I thank You that every thought that keeps me captive has to break and yield, and I do not need to fear. You are the Lord of my mind and You have given me power to win. I thank You for the divine power of Your word to use against wrong attitudes in my mind. Amen.

# Day 25

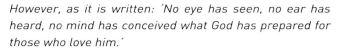

*However, as it is written: 'No eye has seen, no ear has heard, no mind has conceived what God has prepared for those who love him.'*

**1 CORINTHIANS 2:9 NIV**

*'Love the Lord your God with all your heart and with all your soul and with all your mind and with all your strength.'*

**MARK 12:30 NIV**

## Thought of transformation

If we truly analyze the privilege of our relationship with God in detail, it will blow our minds! I still find it so incredible to think that this powerful, awesome God loves and cares for me in such personal detail. He is an amazing God! We need to let the overwhelming revelation of this love of God penetrate our minds. However much we try to rationalize and reason concerning His love, it is totally unfathomable. Not only does He love me today, but He has decided to love me forever and is preparing a future of blessing for me too! His love pursues us, forgives us, restores us and then blesses and provides for us! None of us deserve such dedicated, generous love – it does

blow your mind! This love of God is totally unreasonable but so wonderful!

Then God gives us a challenge: *Will you love me too?* In Mark 12:30 He asks us to love Him and express our love with every part of our being. First we are asked to 'Love the Lord your God will all your soul and heart', which is a more natural place to express our love from. But then the challenge gets deeper: now love the Lord with all your mind! I wonder how I can express my love for this amazing God with my entire mind.

I remember my husband Gordon saying to me early on in our marriage, 'Rachel, I do like it when you tell me you love me, but I get an even greater sense of closeness when you tell me that you really trust me!' Somehow this sincere expression of trust showed Gordon that our relationship was more than a heart connection. I really had thought about our relationship and had decided with my mind that I could trust him.

Do you trust God when circumstances do not make sense? Can your mind process contradictions and still say, 'I love and trust Him'? Ask God today to teach you to deepen your love of Him in your ways of thinking and with your entire mind.

## Prayer of declaration

God, I thank You that Your goodness and plans for me will blow my mind. I thank You that there are times when what You do is beyond understanding. I thank You, God, that You have prepared things for me that are beyond my way of thinking, and they are big because You love me. Father, help me to trust even when I cannot process everything – help me to know Your care even when I feel unable to grasp intellectually all the steps of the journey. Father, teach me to use my mind to love You in a deeper and more profound way. I know that You love me and have planned good things for me, but now let me learn to love You with my entire mind. Father, teach me the spiritual love language of the mind. Let me know that my mind can love God and my mind is not a hindrance to You! Amen.

# Day 26

*I pray that out of his glorious riches he may strengthen you with power through his Spirit in your inner being, so that Christ may dwell in your hearts through faith. And I pray that you, being rooted and established in love, may have power, together with all the saints, to grasp how wide and long and high and deep is the love of Christ, and to know this love that surpasses knowledge – that you may be filled to the measure of all the fullness of God. Now to him who is able to do immeasurably more than all we ask, think or **imagine**, according to his power that is at work within us...*

**EPHESIANS 3:16–20 NIV (EMPHASIS MINE)**

## Thought of transformation

I believe that unless we truly learn this secret of loving God with all our minds, we will never be able to develop our true potential. As this revelation of the love of God touches our lives, it will also awaken our minds to think about ourselves correctly, without our limitations. We begin to see the potential that God sees in us, and then our creativity and imagination are triggered to dream. We are often told that you become like the one you love... so as our love for God deepens, so we will begin to think like Him and start to enter His amazing world of creativity and vision. We need to pray this prayer with Paul and ask God to revolutionize the way we process that love of God in our lives. We need to have a foundational understanding of this love which becomes a reference point for all our decision-making and analysis. We need to know that God is for us and is trustworthy. Unless we are rooted and established in this love, we will always be double-minded, one moment believing and the next moment doubting. We have to be utterly convinced about the goodness of God.

Once we know this love and are firmly rooted in this knowledge, then our lives will become fruitful. For unless our lives are rooted they can never be fruitful! Think of the illustration of a potted plant. You can purchase an apple tree from the garden nursery but if you never plant it in the soil, it will never root properly and so will never produce apples, and in time it will die. In the same way, our lives must be fully rooted in the knowledge of the love of God if we are going to be abundantly fruitful. This fruitfulness will include an ability to think and imagine in cooperation with the Holy Spirit. He will increase your aptitude and you will be amazed at your mental capacity! So love God and then dream like God!

## Prayer of declaration

Father, as I allow the revelation of Your love for
me to go deep and root in my life, I thank You that
this atmosphere provides the safe place for me to
dream again. I thank You that as I rest in Your love,
I can watch God do 'more than I can imagine'. Right
now I ask You to touch my mind – the conscious,
unconscious, semi-conscious and dream parts of
my mind – and breathe on them by the Holy Spirit. I
want to ask You to teach my mind to imagine again.
I trust that as I am secure in Your love, You will stir
my mind and touch it with Your imagination and do
what I cannot do. So, God, touch my mind and let
me imagine. Stir all my creativity. Stir the writer in
me. Stir the thinker and the strategist. Stir my gift
of administration. Lord, let me use my mind for You.
Amen.

# Day 27

*How long must I wrestle with my thoughts and every day have sorrow in my heart? How long will my enemy triumph over me?*

**PSALM 13:2 NIV**

*Search me, O God, and know my heart; test me and know my anxious thoughts.*

**PSALM 139:23 NIV**

*Therefore, holy brothers, who share in the heavenly calling, fix your thoughts on Jesus, the apostle and high priest whom we confess.*

**HEBREWS 3:1 NIV**

## Thought of transformation

Often our mind can become a darkroom where we develop all our negatives of fear and doubt. As we release our mind to dream and imagine once again, we find we have to wrestle for our freedom in our thinking. We need to take every thought captive, especially in our free-thinking time, our dream life and those moments when we are drifting off to sleep. We need to discipline our thought patterns and uproot

all the fears and worry that control our thinking. Ask God to show you how you spend your thinking time. Ask God to reveal to you the thought processes that trap you in fear, bitterness or insecurity.

I have found that I often need to make an active decision to think correctly about difficult situations – otherwise, I get overwhelmed. We need to make the choice to put on some worship music instead of the TV; we need to meditate on a scripture verse rather than an unhelpful conversation. We need to *fix* our thoughts on godly things. Take time to relax before you go to bed and don't start talking about issues that are painful before trying to sleep! We all have seasons when we need to wrestle in our minds, so engage in the battle and win! Think about Jesus and think thoughts that help you win!

## Prayer of declaration

So, Father, I submit all the wrestling in my mind to You. I thank You that this season of struggle will finish. I do not have to suffer in my mind any longer – You have made me free! I thank You that You can search me and find every anxious thought and then

help me to conquer these thoughts. I will sleep at night – I will not be worried about anything. I will not be conquered by bitterness or insecurity any more, but with God I will win. So, Father, right now I choose to fix my thoughts on Jesus. I will focus all I am on Him, and I know I can be free. Father, let my thoughts have a Jesus focus. Thank You for holding me as we fight the battle for my mind. Amen.

# Day 28

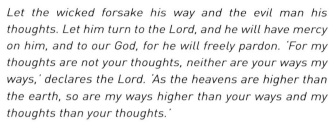

*Let the wicked forsake his way and the evil man his thoughts. Let him turn to the Lord, and he will have mercy on him, and to our God, for he will freely pardon. 'For my thoughts are not your thoughts, neither are your ways my ways,' declares the Lord. 'As the heavens are higher than the earth, so are my ways higher than your ways and my thoughts than your thoughts.'*

**ISAIAH 55:7–9 NIV**

*For the word of God is living and active. Sharper than any double-edged sword, it penetrates even to dividing soul and spirit, joints and marrow; it judges the thoughts and attitudes of the heart.*

**HEBREWS 4:12 NIV**

## Thought of transformation

The more we walk with God, the more we realize that we do not think like God! His ways do not make sense, but they are good. We have to learn to let go and let God lead us in His ways. Our thought processes are so often selfish and inward looking, but God teaches us the bigger picture. His ways will also challenge our perspective and sense of justice. God loves to offend our minds to reveal our heart's motivation.

As we let the word of God touch our lives, it will ruthlessly expose our attitudes and motivations. We often think that we are being generous and selfless, until God challenges us to go another mile or give at another level! His word has the power to penetrate. Recently, God challenged me to give to a project. The amount was significant and meant we would need to sacrifice in other areas of our life, but we gave. When the people concerned did not really thank us or acknowledge the gift, I was amazed at how I struggled with a sense of resentment. I wanted these people to shower us with thanks and acknowledge the generosity and personal cost. I realized I wanted praise! I thought I had given generously, but in reality I had given with strings attached, and I had to repent. God had revealed my heart!

Take a moment to look at the circumstances in your life and see if you have been offended. Take time and allow His word to do its work in your life.

## Prayer of declaration

Father, I thank You for the word of God that can teach me all things. I ask You for a new love and understanding of the power of Your word. I thank You that Your word is able to discern my thoughts. I thank You that Your word can speak to both my mind and my heart, and then teach them to function together. I am redeemed and precious. I know that I am a leader. I thank You for fresh hope and that You can reform my thinking. God, I ask You to deepen my revelation of Your ways. I thank You that Your thoughts are higher than my thoughts, and that although they may not seem logical, they are filled with Your goodness. Help me to turn to You when I cannot understand things. Help me not to depend on my mind to work everything out. Lord, deepen my faith so that I can trust even if I do not understand the journey. Let me feel safe even if I cannot process every step. Let me have a revelation of this scripture in my life: 'As the heavens are higher than the earth, so are My ways higher than Your ways and My thoughts than Your thoughts.' Thank You for Your word. Amen.

## STEPPING STONE 5
# Reawaken Your Dreams

# Day 29

*As the deer pants for streams of water, so my soul pants for you, O God. **My soul thirsts** for God, for the living God. When can I go and meet with God? My tears have been my food day and night, while men say to me all day long, 'Where is your God?' These things I remember as I pour out my soul: how I used to go with the multitude, leading the procession to the house of God, with shouts of joy and thanksgiving among the festive throng. Why are you downcast, O my soul? Why so disturbed within me? Put your hope in God, for I will yet praise him, my Saviour and my God. My soul is downcast within me; therefore I will remember you from the land of the Jordan, the heights of Hermon – from Mount Mizar. **Deep calls to deep** in the roar of your waterfalls; all your waves and breakers have swept over me. By day the Lord directs his love, at night his song is with me – a prayer to the God of my life.*

**PSALM 42:1–8 NIV (EMPHASIS MINE)**

## Thought of transformation

Are you hungrier today for the presence of God in your life than you were last year? Is there a longing to have time with Him? Is there a cry from your depths that shouts, 'I need you, God'? I believe that God

wants to awaken in you a fresh passion for Him. So often, when we feel weary emotionally, we withdraw from God and our Christian friends, and our passion begins to die. But God wants to awaken your passions and dreams. Today, remember how you used to love the atmosphere of God in church, remember the excitement of good worship times, and dream again. Remember those moments of intimacy when you heard the voice of your Father blessing you.

Let those deep places of your being begin to express your desires once again. Do not let the pain and disappointment of yesterday silence your true desires. Let the true intensity of your passion burn once more and allow God to fan into flame the expectation that has died.

There is a part of you that is thirsty for more, and this needs to be satisfied in the presence of God. So seek Him, and find that He is able to awaken what you thought had died, and then allow yourself to dream with God once more!

## Prayer of declaration

Father, just as I have given You my yesterday and my today, so now I give You my tomorrow. I trust You to open the door to my dreams and every longing for tomorrow. I do know that You have *good* plans for me, and so I ask You to stir my desires and longings. Father, where I am afraid of these deep longings, I ask You to hold me safe. I am so thirsty for something more. I so want to break through all the frustration of my spiritual dreams that have got so stuck. Please, God, take me to the next step and satisfy those cries deep inside. God, where I have felt disturbed, I *will* put my hope in You. So, Father, in this atmosphere of Your love, I ask You to open the inner cries and longings of my soul and let deep call to deep. I trust You to awaken the dreams and hopes that are right for this season. Breathe on me, God, and stir the embers of my hope again. Let me dream again! Thank You. Amen.

# Day 30

*Therefore I am now going to allure her; I will lead her into the desert and speak tenderly to her. There I will give her back her vineyards, and will make the Valley of Achor a door of hope. There she will sing as in the days of her youth, as in the day she came up out of Egypt.*

**HOSEA 2:14–15 NIV**

## Thought of transformation

This is a season of restoration. You will discover that gifts that you thought you had lost will reappear and what has seemed so barren will become fruitful. Often the journey of our dreams seems to take a long detour into the desert. We can feel confused, quite certain that we have followed the voice of God, and yet find ourselves in a tough, dry place. But then God will turn these dry places into destiny appointments. Just because life has been difficult does not mean you have been bad or God is mad with you! Often you will find that God draws you with His tender voice, you follow, and then discover that you have landed in a hard place. Why? It is because He wants to establish in your life a new level of authority and trust for a new season of influence!

So, today, listen to the voice of His affirmation and do not be distracted by the barren landscape. God can turn the barren place into a fruitful field in a moment. But we need to learn the lessons of the wilderness if we are ever going to birth our dreams. As you read the Bible, you will notice that every significant leader had a desert encounter. Moses, David, and even Jesus all had to face their battles in the wilderness before they could step into their destiny. If we want to birth our dreams, we will have to learn to conquer the wilderness too.

So remember that we are made for desert combat. We will win and turn the barren place into our fruitful zone. We will walk out of this valley of trouble (Achor) through the door of hope and live our dreams. This is a season of breakthrough when we will find that our dreams will thrive!

## Prayer of declaration

Father, I do trust that You are speaking to me and that Your voice has been leading me. Even though my dreams have been in a wilderness place, I trust You to keep speaking life to me. But I believe that the season of change is coming, and now is the time for me to walk out of this place and through the door of hope. Lord, I have been in a valley of trouble but now I know You have a door of hope for me. I break the power of disappointment over my life and its influence over my capacity to dream. I believe I can know hope. Father, let me sing again, and put a Youthful spirit in me that loves to dream and imagine. Thank You for my early days of dreaming. Now let me walk into this new season. Amen.

# Day 31

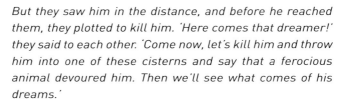

*But they saw him in the distance, and before he reached them, they plotted to kill him. 'Here comes that dreamer!' they said to each other. 'Come now, let's kill him and throw him into one of these cisterns and say that a ferocious animal devoured him. Then we'll see what comes of his dreams.'*

**GENESIS 37:18–20 NIV**

## Thought of transformation

Today we need to recognize the dream-crushers in our lives. Fears, people's expectations and words that have been spoken over us can all limit our destiny. I remember that whilst I was in my early twenties, I was told that I was a poor communicator and that I should never try to speak to youth audiences. For years, any time I had an invitation to speak to youth conferences, I was fearful that I could not do it, although I had many positive words given to me about influencing and leading the next generation. In the end I had to break the influence of those negative words off my life so that I could fulfil my purpose.

We need to recognize that often it is the people close to us – family members or childhood friends –

who can crush our dreams. Like Joseph's brothers, these people are unable to discern the new season and feel threatened or overprotective, and so they try to kill the dreams rather than encourage them. Often family find it hard to endorse your new calling if they feel it conflicts with their idea of a 'nice, safe and respectable' career. Often I have found that if the dream-crusher starts to appear, it is a good indication that the new direction I am sensing is the right one!

As you step out into new horizons, you will discover that you meet new levels of opposition and you have to hold fast to your vision. So do not let the dream-crusher win. You will encounter circumstances that will try to kill the life in your new dreams, but let your dreams live!

## Prayer of declaration

Father, I have anger in my spirit against the plan of the enemy that has tried to kill my dreams. Reveal to me every situation where the atmosphere of the dream-crusher has wounded me. And, Father, I thank You for the power of Your word to set me free. Father, I thank You that however much my circumstances and my pain have tried to crush the dream, You are the God of more than enough. Father, I declare that nothing can kill my God-dreams. You have said it, and so I know You can make a way. So I resist that sound that says, 'We'll see what becomes of her dreams!' God, You know what will become of my dreams, and I trust You to make it happen. Thank You, God, that my dreams are not fruitless. Amen.

# Day 32

*And afterward, I will pour out my Spirit on all people. Your sons and daughters will prophesy, your old men will dream dreams, your young men will see visions. Even on my servants, both men and women, I will pour out my Spirit in those days. I will show wonders in the heavens and on the earth.*

**JOEL 2:28–30 NIV**

## Thought of transformation

When we are soaked by the atmosphere of the Holy Spirit, we begin to dream and think outside of the box. Again and again, when I have attended a conference or retreat time where I have allowed myself to focus on God completely, I have begun to get fresh vision and purpose for the next stage of my life. The atmosphere of the Holy Spirit is like an incubation chamber, and in this place we begin to dream God-sized dreams! As we spend time in God's presence, we come into fresh alignment with the God-purpose that is written on the inside of our life.

What is prophecy? I believe prophecy is declaring the God-dream over a life. It is saying the same thing that God has already said about you. God created the innermost desires and instincts of your nature and He knows what purpose will truly satisfy you. So as we step into the Holy Spirit's atmosphere, these seeds of creation are stirred and come to life. We discover what really matters to us and what purpose we want to give our lives. Prophecy is when we hear God declaring His true purpose for our life, which He designed when He formed us. And this word has the power to awaken our true calling. So when we begin to prophesy in this atmosphere of the Holy Spirit, we are just agreeing with what God has already decreed for our lives. We are beginning to dream what God has already dreamed and see the vision that God has already seen!

We are never too old to birth our dreams – both old men and young men have a dream capacity. So do not let your age limit your ability to incubate new vision. We need to soak ourselves in this incubating chamber of God, and dream with heaven, and then birth the dreams and visions captured while we were in the presence of God. Let God awaken his dream in your life.

## Prayer of declaration

Father, pour out a fresh spirit upon me – let me be wet with the presence of God. Father, blow through my life and awaken the prophetic call upon me. I thank You that You have given me a spirit of revelation and prophecy. I thank You that as I let Your Spirit touch my life, Your calling upon me will grow. I ask You to let me dream God-sized dreams, and see visions. Open up a new heavenly perspective of Your purpose for my life. Come, Holy Spirit, and create in me an atmosphere which stirs the dreamer and increases my revelation. Thank You, Father. Amen.

# Day 33

*'Sing, O barren woman, you who never bore a child; burst into song, shout for joy, you who were never in labour; because more are the children of the desolate woman than of her who has a husband,' says the Lord. 'Enlarge the place of your tent, stretch your tent curtains wide, do not hold back; lengthen your cords, strengthen your stakes. For you will spread out to the right and to the left; your descendants will dispossess nations and settle in their desolate cities. Do not be afraid; you will not suffer shame. Do not fear disgrace; you will not be humiliated. You will forget the shame of your youth and remember no more the reproach of your widowhood. For your Maker is your husband – the Lord Almighty is his name – the Holy One of Israel is your Redeemer; he is called the God of all the earth...'*

**ISAIAH 54:1–5 NIV**

## Thought of transformation

This is a season of acceleration and increase. But to create this environment of fruitfulness, we need to sing about it before we can see it! Here God promises that we will enter into a new place of influence and expansion, but first we need to learn to sing when

it is still a barren time. This very act of faith – having an attitude of gratitude and thanksgiving even when nothing appears to be happening – begins the process of change. There is great power in praise and thanksgiving offered in the tough times, even before we can see any proof that God will provide for us.

First we need to sing about this new season, and then we need to take our ground and enlarge and move into the new position. We need to go through those times of enlarging, stretching, spreading out until we can feel afraid and overstretched. When we make steps of faith that require serious money to be released, we can feel stretched, but as we allow these seasons of challenge, we discover that we will not be humiliated nor suffer shame. Unless there is a constant risk factor in our lives, we are not really living on the edge of our dreams and pressing into new kingdom territory. God wants you to stretch into your dreams.

Just as when you become pregnant you find your body stretches and enlarges to accommodate the birthing of the new life, so we need to allow our routines and lives to stretch and enlarge to accommodate the new dreams and destiny that God wants to birth. It is time to live outside of our comfort zones. But even though it feels uncomfortable and at times can feel dangerous, God is faithful and will provide the people, resources and money to build his dream projects.

Now is the time to sing your way out of the barren season and to allow God to stretch you into His plans. You will then discover that He is a faithful God who provides all that you need.

## Prayer of declaration

Father, I thank You that in the place where I have felt such barrenness, I will know a new stretching. Father, I will not be fearful. Instead I will *sing*, as I know that there is a stretching and enlarging that will satisfy every dream and calling. Father, I declare that I will stretch out, and that the place of limitation is lifting, and that You are doing a new thing in my life. I thank You that these dreams will not humiliate me but will satisfy me. I thank You that this time I will not feel isolated and alone, but You will give me relationships and You will be with me. I am covered and sheltered. I can stretch out! Thank You for my song of thanksgiving. Amen.

# Day 34

> *The angel answered, 'The Holy Spirit will come upon you,*
> *and the power of the Most High will overshadow you... For*
> *nothing is impossible with God.'*
>
> *'I am the Lord's servant,' Mary answered. 'May it be*
> *to me as you have said.'*
>
> *... [Elizabeth exclaimed:] 'Blessed is she who*
> *has believed that what the Lord has said to her will be*
> *accomplished!'*

**LUKE 1:35, 37–38, 45 NIV**

> *And without faith it is impossible to please God, because*
> *anyone who comes to him must believe that he exists and*
> *that he rewards those who earnestly seek him.*

**HEBREWS 11:6 NIV**

## Thought of transformation

When God shares His dreams with you, they always
feel impossible and seem ridiculous. Here was Mary,
being promised a child without even having sexual
intercourse! The whole situation was impossible, but
Mary was able to see beyond reality into the world of
God's possibility. Today, as you meditate on your God
dreams, let the Holy Spirit overshadow your doubts

and fear with His presence and sense of security. For when God steps into our lives, impossible things become possible. I remember when I was first asked to write a book, it seemed an *impossible* task. I struggled to write the simplest essay at school, so how could I write a book?! But then God gave me a public prophetic word, clearly stating that he wanted me to write, so I believed this word and began to write. As I did so, faith began to grow until the task was accomplished. In fact, when I finished my first book, I sat and cried. Impossible things had become possible!

Ask God to mix faith with your dreams. Everything we accomplish can only please God if our activity has been mixed with faith, rather than our determined willpower to make it happen. We need to be believers who position ourselves to be good receivers of all of God's provision, to help us achieve our dreams. When everything screams in our face, 'This can never happen!', we need to be those who scream back, 'This cannot help but happen!'

I love the story told about when Napoleon was in the midst of one of his fiercest battles. One of his officers came to him and reported that the enemy had them surrounded on three flanks and asked if he would speak to the troops. So Napoleon stood up and said, 'Men, we are surrounded on the left, we are surrounded on the right, the enemy is in front of us

and the enemy is behind us. Men, let us fight — we cannot miss!'

Sometimes we can feel so surrounded by the impossibilities, but when Goliath is so big, remember that he is a giant you cannot miss when you throw the rock of faith!

## Prayer of declaration

Father, I ask for a new spirit of trust and faith. I do believe! I break the power of doubt and insecurity. I know many things seem impossible, but I want to believe that You are the God of miracles and You love me and will position me to accomplish what You have asked me to do. Like Mary,  I will see amazing breakthrough and I will hold my impossible dreams. Thank You for the word of faith that will accomplish victory. Amen.

# STEPPING STONE 6
## Revive Your Life

# Day 35

*The thief comes only to steal and kill and destroy; I have come that they may have life, and have it to the full.*

**JOHN 10:10 NIV**

*The Lord God formed the man from the dust of the ground and breathed into his nostrils the breath of life, and the man became a living being.*

**GENESIS 2:7 NIV**

## Thought of transformation

Life is meant to be lived and not just admired. Often in my job I meet young, attractive girls who have become convinced that they are ugly, too fat or lacking purpose. In the worst cases they have

begun to think about suicide, or they may self-harm or suffer with anorexia or other health issues. As I look at these outstanding young people and see how the enemy has trapped them in a web of lies so that they have been robbed of the joy of life, I feel such a sense of anger against this thief. We do have an enemy and he loves to destroy our sense of well-being and life. He steals and tries to kill that God-given gift of our future and seeks to destroy our passion to live life fully.

But when we allow God to refocus our life, He gives us back the ability to live life to the full! He has come to give us a complete, satisfied, overflowing life. So, we must take back our life from the grip of this thief and learn to live our life to the full.

So, today, identify those areas where the thief has stolen your love of life and ask God to refresh you. Just as in that first day, God wants to breathe his breath into the depth of your life so that you can live a complete life. It is only when we carry his breath in our spirit that we can truly live our life. So let Him breathe into your nostrils the breath of life, and become a living being once again. It is time to really live, laugh and dance!

## Prayer of declaration

God, I thank You that You gave me a life that should be fun and carefree. My life should not be stressful and pressured – You give me the ability to *live* life! Thank You so much that You come and give me life! Father, today I receive this life – this full, overflowing, wonderful life. You are so good to me. Today I ask You to destroy all the negativity in my life. Breathe into me again. Breathe into every area of dust. Wake up the real 'me' and let me become the living being You created me to be. I rebuke the thief and all his work in my life. Father, breathe into me. Today I declare, 'I am alive – I am free!' Thank You for this gift of life. Amen.

# Day 36

*Will you not revive us again, that your people may rejoice in you?*

**PSALM 85:6 NIV**

*For this is what the high and lofty One says – he who lives forever, whose name is holy: 'I live in a high and holy place, but also with him who is contrite and lowly in spirit, to revive the spirit of the lowly and to revive the heart of the contrite...'*

**ISAIAH 57:15 NIV**

*After two days he will revive us; on the third day he will restore us, that we may live in his presence.*

**HOSEA 6:2 NIV**

## Thought of transformation

God promises to come and revive us and awaken all that we fear may have died permanently. He can renew our first love, refresh our spirit and refocus our vision. God is able to cause us to rejoice so that we feel the sense of laughter rise up once again. God loves to revitalize our dreams and passion.

So often when we speak about 'revival' we

imagine huge meetings with powerful preaching of the word and sick people getting healed. Although this is one expression of God, he also promises that he brings revival to those who are lowly. Who are the lowly? The lowly are those who are simple, ordinary, common, modest or humble. So that gives most of us a hope of revival! It is our desperation that attracts the presence of God in our life more than our perfection. I am reminded of the simple prayer that Evan Roberts prayed before revival hit Wales. He just cried, 'Lord, bend me – bend me!' Often our times of frustration lead us into a godly desperation that then triggers a season of revelation that will birth transformation. So do not be afraid to release your cry: 'Revive me – touch me, Lord!'

Then God promises us that after a delay, He will revive us. He will touch those desperate places and put back life and hope. So do not fear this season of waiting. Waiting time is never wasted time. The season of revival will come, but just wait for it! Just dwell on these scriptures and let them become a cry for Him – the giver of life!

## Prayer of declaration

Father, I thank You for the spirit of revival that will rest on me. Revive me and all that has died inside

– revive me, God! Father, I thank You that as I call upon Your name, You hear my cry and You awaken me. Thank You, Father, that where I feel crushed and broken, You revive me. Let me know Your touch and let me live in Your presence. Revive me, God. Amen.

# Day 37

*From there they continued on to Beer, the well where the Lord said to Moses, 'Gather the people together and I will give them water.' Then Israel sang this song: 'Spring up, O well!...'*

**NUMBERS 21:16–17 NIV**

*On the last and greatest day of the Feast, Jesus stood and said in a loud voice, 'If anyone is thirsty, let him come to me and drink. Whoever believes in me, as the Scripture has said, streams of living water will flow from within him.'*

**JOHN 7:37–38 NIV**

## Thought of transformation

As we learn to come to the source of life, we will in turn become a resource to others. First God fills us up and then we can pour out and refresh others. So we must examine our water source to make sure it is good water! When we have been through a pressured season of life, this can either make us bitter or better able to face our next challenge. If we have allowed bitterness to contaminate our thinking and reactions, our well will be blocked. So we will need to unblock this well with praise and thanksgiving. So many

different rocks and offences can block our life-flow and stifle our destiny, so we need to sing to our well of life and activate our destiny!

I remember when I went through a hurtful time of betrayal, my water source got blocked. I had to make a conscious decision to forgive and release the sense of injustice before I could find peace and the water began to flow again. Ask God to show you if you have stones of unforgiveness that are blocking your life-flow.

Now come to God and drink. We need to just stop and allow God to fill us. This is a process of reflection and contemplation, where we just stop talking and let God touch us. Let all your frustration draw you to Jesus and ask Him to give you fresh water. There is nothing better than learning to rest in the presence of God and then drinking from Him. As we come, we will get wet with the presence of God and He will fill us. Then we will find that the wilderness place within has been transformed and suddenly there are streams of water flowing again.

I remember after a time of persecution at school, I was worried about letting people know I loved Jesus, so I closed down all my passion for Him. But one night as I worshipped in a service, I found my old love being reawakened. Suddenly, I found I was praying for my schoolfriends again. Soon I was bringing them to church and was seeing them get saved and baptized. The well was unblocked and the water was flowing again!

## Prayer of declaration

Father, from deep inside of me I ask You to fill me – spring up, O well! Let a new song of hunger flow from within me. O God, spring up! Father, I confess that I am thirsty and I need You so much. I need the touch of Your presence – teach me to drink of Your life. God, not only do I want to know life within me, but I so long to be a life-giver. I want there to be an overflow of life from me. I do not want to survive – I want to thrive. Thank You, Father, that life will come forth! I believe that streams of life will flow from me and touch the nations. I believe that life flows from me for people. More water, Lord, I pray! Amen.

# Day 38

*With long life will I satisfy him and show him my salvation.*

**PSALM 91:16 NIV**

*The Lord will guide you always; he will satisfy your needs in a sun-scorched land and will strengthen your frame. You will be like a well-watered garden, like a spring whose waters never fail.*

**ISAIAH 58:11 NIV**

*'... I will refresh the weary and satisfy the faint.'*
*At this I awoke and looked around. My sleep had been pleasant to me.*

**JEREMIAH 31:25–26 NIV**

## Thought of transformation

We should live a satisfied life with few regrets! I love the story told of John Wesley on his deathbed. The story goes that a good friend came to visit him and asked him, 'John, if you had your life again, what would you do differently?' Apparently Wesley rolled over in his bed and looked at his friend and replied, 'Nothing – *satisfied*!' What a wonderful thing to be

able to say at the end of your life. Life had not been easy for Wesley – he had endured many physical hardships and had had a difficult marriage. But he was still able to look at the overall result of his life and conclude that he was satisfied. I want that to be my testimony too, and I do believe that it can be! God wants to give you satisfaction emotionally, practically and spiritually.

God can satisfy us in every area of our life. I believe that God will satisfy us with good relationships. He will direct our life's decisions, helping us to make wise choices. And He will provide for us even when we are living in a time of financial uncertainty. The kingdom of God is not affected by economic disasters or credit crises. Whatever the atmosphere in the workplace, God can enable you to live life satisfied and give you strength to face every challenge. Even when you fear bad news, or are concerned about health issues, God still has a way of providing grace and strength so that you can feel refreshed and have a bubble of joy on the inside, even if life is tough on the outside!

I remember the period of eight months when I was confined to a wheelchair; it was difficult but not traumatic. Somehow in the midst of all the pain and frustration, God still watered my soul. He showed me His care in a hundred little ways each day, and I knew that He was with me.

So, today, know that God refreshes you and will satisfy you to the depth of your being. It is time to live life satisfied!

## Prayer of declaration

God, I thank You that with You I can look at my
life and be satisfied. No regrets – You satisfy! You
will satisfy me in my relationships. You
will satisfy me in my ministry.
You will satisfy me in my
circumstances – You are
the God who satisfies! I
thank You that You will
satisfy me with practical
provision – I do not need
to fear. I thank You that
You will satisfy me with
long life. You will refresh
me and remove weariness
and satisfy me with good
sleep! Thank You for all
Your care for me. Amen!

# Day 39

*Now I am about to go the way of all the earth. You know
with all your heart and soul that not one of all the good
promises the Lord your God gave you has failed. Every
promise has been fulfilled; not one has failed.*

**JOSHUA 23:14 NIV**

*Your promises have been thoroughly tested, and your
servant loves them.*

**PSALM 119:140 NIV**

*Your kingdom is an everlasting kingdom, and your dominion
endures through all generations. The Lord is faithful to all
his promises and loving toward all he has made.*

**PSALM 145:13 NIV**

## Thought of transformation

We can live life knowing that every promise of God is
true and will happen. But in my experience, God does
not necessarily fulfil the promises in the order we
would choose or even in the order in which we received
them! It often seems that the promise we want most
is the last to appear. But we need to know that every
time we receive a promise, it is secured in the bank

of heaven and it will be credited to our account.

The other challenge is often that our promises seem to go backward before they go forward! In other words, it seems that the situation gets worse before it gets better. I was praying with a friend about her work situation, which had become very pressurized, as she worked for a boss who was ultra-demanding. Then the next week my friend was told she was being moved to a different department, and she was delighted. But when she started work there, it appeared that everything was ten times worse. The atmosphere was tense and there was an ongoing disciplinary hearing concerning one of the staff. But just before she moved, God had given her a word: 'Get ready for significant promotion and the job of your dreams!' She was in this new department for six months and thought about resigning every day, but she could not let go of her promise. Then suddenly one day she got an email saying, 'We want to move you and wonder if you would be prepared to do this job.' It had the exact specifications of her dreams, and although she was not experienced enough for the position, she was given it, and she has loved her work ever since!

So remember – His promises are trustworthy. Now is not a good time to give up, but hold fast to every word and watch and see. His promises will come true!

## Prayer of declaration

Father, thank You that Your promises are good and never fail. I believe that *every* promise will be fulfilled so that I can know abundant life. You will satisfy me with good things. I am so excited to see how all the promises over my life will break through. I thank You for every promise and every

prophetic word. Help me to treasure each word. I thank You for strength for every test and for help to know that Your promises will win the day. They will break through. I know You are faithful and Your promises are a secure foundation for my life. Amen.

# Day 40

*And the glory of the Lord will be revealed, and all mankind together will see it. For the mouth of the Lord has spoken.*

**ISAIAH 40:5 NIV**

*So do not throw away your confidence; it will be richly rewarded. You need to persevere so that when you have done the will of God, you will receive what he has promised. For in just a very little while, 'He who is coming will come and will not delay. But my righteous one will live by faith. And if he shrinks back, I will not be pleased with him.' But we are not of those who shrink back and are destroyed, but of those who believe and are saved. Now faith is being sure of what we hope for and certain of what we do not see.*

**HEBREWS 10:35 – 11:1 NIV**

## Thought of transformation

As you complete these stepping stones, take a moment to remember each word that God has spoken to you. Remember that these words came from the mouth of God, so they will be fulfilled. It is incredible to think that when the mouth of God speaks, something must happen. As you step off these stepping stones onto the new pathway of your life, remember that you are a glory carrier. The presence of God has touched your life and you are beautiful. You have a purpose and the grace of leadership to reach your goal. You have dreams and a hope growing inside your spirit. You have an intelligent mind that will help you focus and make good decisions. So get ready to live life satisfied. Carry your new glory and live a satisfied life full of joy!

Do not let anything rob you of this new confidence. This is the season of new beginnings. There will be new opportunities and doors in front of you, so open them and watch God provide for you every step of the way. Remember that often these decisions will require steps of courage, so do not shrink back. Remember to press through each difficulty and win. Let this new hope and faith arise. Walk out into your world, head up and shoulders back, knowing that God is with you. You are a precious princess or prince, valued by your Father, so go and live your life to the full.

## Prayer of declaration

Father, I thank You that this is the time for my life to be revealed. Everything is being released and You are revealing who I am. I thank You that the glory of God will be revealed in me. I thank You that my destiny will be revealed. I thank You that as I come as a little child, I will know the secrets of heaven. I am ready.

So, today, I declare I am a child of faith and I will see my dreams come true. This has been a birthing season and now I will see and hold my promises. Thank You, God! So I dare to dream, knowing that You and I together have the power to make dreams come true. My life is in Your hands and my future is secure. My life will be wonderful. I am free... I am free... I am free to be completely me!

I know that I am redeemed and precious. I believe that I have rediscovered the leader who has been reluctant – she (or he) will step forth. I have reclaimed my hope. God has reformed my thinking and I am free in my mind. Now is the time to reawaken my dreams. Now is the day to let revival touch my life. I am free! Thank You, my precious Father. *Amen.*

## DARE TO DREAM!

*'Dare to dream,' says the Lord,*
*'for in dreaming you share My heart.*
*Dare to dream,' says the Lord,*
*'for without a dream people perish.*
*Many set their sights too low,*
*many lack the faith to try.*
*Many seeds I sow in hearts,*
*Even share My own heart's cry.*
*Dare to dream, I will you on.*
*Dare to dream for I dream with you.*
*Can you, will you, dare to dream?*
*Can you, will you, catch My vision?*
*Will you let the seeds bear fruit?*
*Will your heartbeat echo Mine?'*

**HELEN AZER, 2 FEBRUARY 2004**

## About the Author

Rachel Hickson is an internationally respected prayer leader and Bible teacher with a recognized prophetic gift. She teaches all over the world, and is in demand as a conference speaker.

At the age of twenty-four Rachel, with her husband Gordon, worked alongside Reinhard Bonnke and the Christ for All Nations team in Africa. After just six weeks in Zimbabwe she almost lost her life in a horrific car accident, but was miraculously healed by God. This incident birthed in Rachel a desire to pray and to train others to realize the full potential of a praying church.

After returning from Africa in 1990, Rachel and Gordon pastored a group of four churches in Hertfordshire, and it was during this time that they established Heartcry Ministries, with the call to train and equip people to be released into effective prayer and intercession for their communities, cities and nations. In 2005 Rachel and Gordon moved to Oxford, where Gordon is Associate Minister on the staff of St Aldate's Church.

Rachel travels internationally, visiting Europe, North America, Africa and India. Invitations come from various denominational backgrounds, where a passion for unity has brought the churches together to pray for a move of God in their area. Rachel and Gordon have a passion to see cities transformed through the power of prayer and evangelism. One of their projects links churches and prayer ministries across London, which has developed a city strategy called the London Prayernet (see www.londonprayer.net).

Rachel has been married to Gordon for over twenty-seven years and they have two children: their daughter, Nicola, who is married to Tim Douglass, who is on the staff of Hillsong Church in Sydney, Australia; and their son, David, who is studying in the United Kingdom.

## Heartcry Ministries and Heartcry for Change

We work with churches and people from many nations and denominations to equip them in the following areas:

> *Prayer:* Training an army of ordinary people in Prayer Schools and seminars to become confident to break the sound barrier and pray informed, intelligent and passionate prayers.
>
> *Prophetic:* Equipping the church to be an accurate prophetic voice in the nation by teaching in training schools and conferences the principles of the prophetic gift. We seek to train people who are passionate to know the presence of God, to be available to hear His voice and then to speak His word with accuracy so that lives can be touched and changed.
>
> *Women:* Delivering a message of hope to women across the nations and cultures to help them arise with a new confidence so that they can be equipped and ready to fulfil their destiny and execute their kingdom purpose.
>
> *Capital cities:* Standing in the capital cities of the world, working with government institutions, businesses and the church, and then crying out for a new

alignment of the natural and spiritual government in these places. A cry for London and beyond. See www. londonprayer.net

*Business and finance:* Connecting business people with their kingdom purpose, so that provision can partner more effectively with vision and accelerate the purpose of God in nations. Connecting commerce, community and church for change!

*Leaders of tomorrow:* Mentoring and encouraging younger leaders to pioneer the next move of God in the areas of politics and government, social action and justice issues, creative arts and media and the ministry.

*Nations:* Partnering with nations in Africa, the Middle East and India by supplying teaching, training and practical resources to strengthen and equip them as they work for breakthrough in their nations.

*Media, TV and satellite:* Developing training materials to equip and disciple the church in the nations to understand and fulfil their responsibility. To be a voice of encouragement through TV into the homes of the army of ordinary people praying for impossible situations.

*Resources and conferences:* To write books, manuals and training materials that will equip the church to be prepared. To provide conferences and training days where leaders and the church can be encouraged to continue in their purpose and calling.

Heartcry hopes to continue strengthening the church to connect with their community whilst encouraging the people to hear the urgent call to prayer. Now is the time to pray and cry out for our land and continent and watch what God will do for us!

Heartcry Ministries
PO Box 737
Oxford, Oxon
OX1 9FA
UK

www.heartcry.co.uk
www.londonprayer.net